To: Milroy & Kate, may H
continue to bless you

Wong
3/28/04

PARENTING FROM A CHRISTIAN PERSPECTIVE

A Superb Handbook for Successful Living

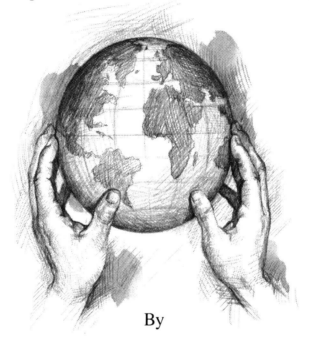

By

Robert H. Givons D.Min

Bloomington, IN Milton Keynes, UK

AuthorHouse™
1663 Liberty Drive, Suite 200
Bloomington, IN 47403
www.authorhouse.com
Phone: 1-800-839-8640

AuthorHouse™ *UK Ltd.*
500 Avebury Boulevard
Central Milton Keynes, MK9 2BE
www.authorhouse.co.uk
Phone: 08001974150

© 2007 Robert H. Givons D.Min. All rights reserved.

No part of this book may be reproduced, stored in a retrieval system, or transmitted by any means without the written permission of the author.

First published by AuthorHouse 2/22/2007

ISBN: 978-1-4259-6735-2 (sc)

Printed in the United States of America
Bloomington, Indiana

This book is printed on acid-free paper.

Acknowledgements

This book and I owe a great deal of gratitude to many people for the extraordinary contribution and co-operation from inception to completion.

I thank my Lord and Savior Jesus Christ who continues to give me strength and vision to do His will.

My children, Patrick, Roan, Natalie, and DeSean, words are not enough to express my gratitude to you so I will simply say this, "I love you all."

My parents, Lascelles Givons and Sis. Gladys (Stepmother) (Deceased). Dad, thank you for being the greatest dad.

My brothers and sisters, Oama, Sugar, Chippy, Les and Moses: Shirley and Marcia thank you all for your inspiration and support.

Dr. Holness and all the members of Central Christian Church, I thank you all for your prayers.

To my dear wife, Michelle I put you last because I need enough space for you. Without you this would not be possible, your insights and substantive contributions are well appreciated. Not only did you provide emotional support but also professional support.

Your frequent and substantive support prevented many errors and mistakes. Thank you, I love you.

NB. To all those who contributed direct and indirectly, may the Lord continue to bless you richly.

Contents

	Introduction	ix
1	Biblical Qualities of Parents	1
2	The Ideal Christian Home	7
3	Parent's Nature	11
4	C-H-I-L-D-R-E-N	15
5	Children are Gifts	21
6	Teach Them Good Manners	25
7	Open Line Communications	29
8	Disciple and Sparing the Rod	33
9	God's Purpose for Marriage	37
10	Divorce	43
11	Co-parental Relationship	49
12	Fathers	51
13	Boys to Men	55
14	Father's Day	59

15	The Joy of Being a Godly Dad	61
16	Responsibilities of Mothers to Daughters	67
17	Godly Parents make a big Difference	73
18	How a God fearing Family should function	77
19	Are the Children really our Future	79
20	Children don't come with Manual	81
21	Taking Parenthood Seriously	85
22	Defiling our Children	89
23	Raising Up or Growing Up	91
24	Taking a Manly Stand	95
25	Faithful Partners	97
26	Legacy of Parents	99
27	Bringing the Family Back	103
28	References	107

Introduction

Families are the building blocks of our society and are the most important investment in our children. Parents should create experiences that foster core values, family values, great character qualities, and strong relationship; when these are adapted in the every day lives, will of a certain change the way the world looks in the future, but never forget the Lord our God who lays the foundation for our families.

This is what this book is all about. -Parenting from a Christian perspective. As a youngster growing up, this writer use to sing this song, "If Jesus is in the family what a happy home, What a happy home" can you envision all the homes in your neighborhood in which each parent is a Christ-liked person. This neighborhood would be full of love for each other, no lying, no envying, no malice, no murder and of course no gun crimes.

Wouldn't it be a wonderful thing if more family members would accept Christ in their hearts, parent to child, sister to brother then members of the community live as one big happy family.

This writer makes reference to this very important and profound text, Proverbs 22:6. "Train up a child in the way he should go: and when he is old, he will not depart from it"[1]

Some people are of the opinion that the way a child is going to turn out is determined by environment, with parenting accounting for little in the way of the child success or failure in life.

Others are of the opinion that the way a child is going to turn out is determined by environment, with parents being almost the sole determining factor in how a child is developed, or with the parents still having no real impact on how a child become an adult because of the overwhelming effect of school, friends and of the fall lineup of television programs.

This writer believes, there are various factors involved in how your child turns out. That part of the equation, which is related to heredity, cannot be denied. That the child's life dictates his destiny. But what part will play as an instrument in God's hands to raise your child to be the adult he or she will become?

When Solomon wrote "train up a child in the way he should go" he was referring to a process of parenting that is far more involved than just telling a child what you want him to do. The child needs love compassion, care, guidance, correction and both godly parents.

The parenting process requires taking initiative with your children, not back peddling and reacting to your child's aggressive curiosity. You are suppose to know where the child should end up, thereby enabling you to run ahead of him, planning for his eventual arrival at the various milestone of life.

The notion that you should just sit and watch a child grow up, making sure that he is properly fed and clothed is a severely distorted approach to raising children. That would lead to abandonment of your God given responsibilities.

Can parents guarantee that their children will get converted? No. Your child is responsible for his own soul. But when all is said and

---

[1] All Biblical reference will be quoted from the KJV.

done do you want to be one of those parent that did not do all you could to lay that foundation as you humanly could in raising that child? I hope you do not.

Selected Scriptures

- Proverbs 22:6

Chapter 1

Biblical Qualities of Parents.

As you may have known by now, Scriptures are filled with various references about parenting. Many characters in the Bible who were parents themselves, gave important and exemplary examples of what parenthood is all about.

As a parent my self, I am aware that parenting is very difficult, and at times impossible. After several years at this, one thought one will be perfect at parenting, sad to say this is not true. At times, you appear to be the bad guys when you are the disciplinarian and tyrant. It is also difficult to balance the role of father or mother, friend, rule-maker and rule-enforcer, while simultaneously struggling to understand what is expected of you as a parent.

The strategies of parenting the younger children are different for the teenagers and of course do not work for adulthood.

So what is a parent to do? Often times parents are faced with situations that they were never planned for or had never experienced themselves and have no clue how to approach them. Everything we buy comes with users manual, children do not.

The Bible, God's greatest love story to children is the only book that comes close to teach parenting. As a child, nothing was more important to me than hearing Bible stories. It is widely agreed that it is a tremendous and valuable book of instruction, it teaches us how to live, behave, love, carry each others burdens, and how to be good stewards and parents. It is a known fact that the role of the parent is a difficult and serious one. With juvenile delinquency rates so alarmingly high, teen suicide rampant, criminal violence at an all time high, immorality and peer pressure etc. children need their parents more than ever.

It is said that parents should be their children's best friends. It is important to have a friendly relationship with your children but never forget being their parents is vital. Best friends are easily found, they speaks the language you want to hear, they are also on your side, they will laugh at your immoral jokes, go places and have fun.

Parenting on the other hand is to the contrary. Parents have to teach, guide, provide and care like no other friend would. Parents have the rights and responsibilities to correct their children when they are wrong, friends cannot because the relationship will be hurt, and they cannot hurt your best buddies.

The biblical qualities should be evident and practiced in the home with special emphasis on the father because fathers are the head of the household. Father's impression should be indicatives of God's presence as such a greater burden is placed on the shoulders of the father. In the eyes of children, fathers should be seen as God's representations in their lives.

As previously stated, there are numerous references throughout the Scriptures regarding parenting. The following is a brief list of passages and it's meanings for proper parenting.

1. Proverbs 1:8-9.

My son, hear the instruction of your father,
And do not forsake the law of your mother;
For they will be a graceful ornament on your head,
And chains about your neck.

The instructions or teachings of parents to children are an adornment and things of beauty which are to be cherished. So then, as parents, our responsibilities are great and awesome. We have to take special care of what we teach our children. These instructions begin at home.

2. Proverbs 4. 1

Hear, my children, the instruction of a father.
And give attention to know understanding.

This passage must be read over and over again.

Children are admonished to hear their parents. There are valuable lessons for both father and mother alike. By teaching these important valuable lessons of wisdom and understanding which can only be found in the Lord, children will be able to discern good from evil.

3. Proverbs 13:24

He who spares his rod hates his son,
But he who loves him disciplines him promptly.

Discipline is a very important aspect of parenting. The rod here is used as a metaphor for discipline; do not abuse your children. If you do not discipline your children you do not love them. Spanking children is necessary at times but never to be done in anger. Just as God discipline his own when they get out of line, the same is true of parent to children, because He loves us, He corrects us when we are wrong. (Prov. 3:12)

4. Proverbs 17:6

*Children are the crown of old men
And the glory of children is their father.*

The Biblical value and glory of grandchildren and the value of parents to their children is emphasized in the text above. It is in this union that the bond of greatness contains and preserved generations after generations.

5. Proverbs 22:6

*Train up a child in the way he should go,
And when he is old he will not depart from it.*

This is one of the most profound texts you will read in Scripture. As we teach our children the love of God, wisdom, understanding and compassion, as they grow these good character qualities will be instilled in them. Let us never forget that as we raise our children, they too will seek to raise theirs the same way. When parents provide strong Biblical qualities, good qualities are expected in return also and it is likely that a pattern will be developed for the coming generations, because as we grow these qualities will not depart from the things learned.

6. Proverbs 23:24-25.

The father of the righteous will greatly rejoice, and he who begets a wise child will delight in him. Let your father and your mother be glad, and let her who bored you rejoice,

My father usually makes this comment, "I wish to see the day when all of my children accept the Lord as their personal savior," being the parent of a child who loves the Lord must be a glorious thing. There is no greater joy for a parent than to see their children following the Lord.

7. Matt. 18:6-7.

Whoever cause one of these little ones who believe in me to stumble, it would be better for him if a millstone were hung around his neck, and he were drowned in the depth of the sea. 7. Woe to the world because of offenses! For offense must come, but woe to that man by whom the offenses came.

There is a lesson here from Jesus, parents should know this. Causing a child to or allowing such one to sin is a very serious sin in itself. So then when adults cause a child to commit a sin there are grave consequences.

8. Ephesians 5:1-2:

Therefore be imitators of God as dear children. And walk in love. As Christ also has loved us and given Himself for us, an offering and a sacrifice to God for a sweet-smelling aroma.

We are imitators of God, in the eyes of children; we are to be like Christ, to love them unconditionally. Always remembering that children only listen to 5% of all that we say and watch 95% of what we do.

9. Ephesians 6:1-3.

"Children, obey your parents in the Lord, for this is right. Honor Your father and mother, which is the first commandment with promise: that it may be well with you and you may live long on the earth."

We need not explain these profound words, they are self-explanatory. What are you teaching your children? Do they have a reason to obey you? Think on these things for a while.

The one thing we can truly count on as parents is that at times we will probably mess up. We will say things we probably shouldn't have or we will either be too hard or soft on our children. But if we truly work together, and work honestly to provide a Christ-like example to our children; "teaching the way, the truth and the life," (John 14:6) that is found in Christ Jesus, we will be the parents God has commanded us to be. Through prayers, and with strength, guidance and wisdom provided to us by the Holy Spirit, parenting becomes an exciting experience. At times it seems difficult but with God it becomes a whole lot easier.

Selected Scriptures

- Proverbs 1: 8-9
- Proverbs 4:4ff
- Proverbs 13:24
- Proverbs 17:6
- Proverbs 22:6
- Proverbs 23:23-25
- Matthew 18:6-7
- Ephesians 5:1-2
- Ephesians 6:1-3
- St.John 14:6

Chapter 2

The Ideal Christian Home.

There is no such thing as the "perfect home", well I haven't seen one yet, but there is a very high degree of success in the efforts of parents who maintain a real Christian home. What ever success we may have is ours only by the grace of God. The Christian home should be an example for all to see and learn from. In light of this, the following should be true for the "ideal Christian home."

- Parents should make themselves worthy of respect. This is necessary in a God pleasing relationship.
- Be kind, tender-hearted and forbearing toward each other, giving love to receive love.
- Couples should settle disagreements privately, outside of the hearing of those who are not concern.
- Cherish the Lord in the hearts and homes, and live as in the presence of the Holy Spirit.
- Create an atmosphere which encourages love and peace at all times.

The Christian home cannot function effectively without devotion. The guidelines are as follows.

"Let the Word of Christ dwell in you richly," Col.3:16
- Family members must pray often and earnestly for each other.
- Pray at meal time.
- Observe family worship at least once per week.
- Parents must take turns in Bible reading and praying.
- Pray with and for our children.
- Teach children how to pray
- Teach children how to cultivate a religious life.
- Teach children reverence to God and His holiness.

"Bring them up in the nurture and admonition of the Lord," Eph.6:4
- Our children needs spiritual guidance, therefore, they should participate actively in religious training.
- They must be taught to honor and obey Father and Mother.
- Parents should not provoke children to wrath.
- Do not call them names to do harm but motivate them in the fear of the Lord.
- Harsh treatment and rebuke can be a barrier to gain there confidence.
- Be firm and assertive but never lose your temper
- Try to gain their confidence so that they will come to you for guidance in the time of trouble.
- Apply gospel and law where necessary.
- Know your children, remembering that each one has his or her own characteristics and learning abilities.
- Love them.
- Treat them as you would like to be treated and most of all treat them the way Christ would treat them.

Selected Scriptures

- Colossians 3:16
- Ephesians 6:14

Notes

Chapter 3

Parent's Nature.

It is the nature of parents to love their children. As a parent I noticed that when our children were small, diligent attention were given to their needs, the best of care were given to them. I was always happy with their growth and happiness.

When they were sick, we spare no effort, day and night to nurse them back to good health. We took great pleasure in seeing them accomplish worthwhile objectives in life. These are the advantages of parenthood and parents have an obligation to direct their children.

Parents should be Christians, living by the Bible and portraying an exemplary life before their children, a model life we wish our children to pattern later.

Genesis 8: 21b states as follows, "the existence of a man's heart is evil from childhood", (KVJ) so it is very important that training and teaching begin early in life.

It has been said, "children learn more by observation than through instruction". Therefore, the future happiness and destiny of children depends upon the teaching and knowledge gained. Teaching and living the Ten Commandments is not a matter that we can face with lack of interest.

Parents who are not concerned and who live ungodly lives will have bad effects upon their children in most cases. However, when a sinner repents, the judgment on sin is removed and God forgives him.

It is true that many children suffer mentally and physically because of ungodly parents. It is also true that blessings follows generations of God-fearing parents. The influence that parents have for good or evil is greater than they realize. Parents who are not Christian, who do not worship God, do not read the Bible and have no family worship in their homes, are not doing their duties before God and their children. Parents need to be alert to evil spirits that will influence children. Evil spirits are subtle and destructive and will try to control a young child's heart. Whenever these are established in a child's life, they are very difficult to control.

Unruly spirits are rampant in today's world. It becomes evident at an early age in children's heart that there are spirits of pride, anger and envy, so it is important that parents possess the Spirit of God, so that Satan's work can be discerned and dealt with in time. Oftentimes children manifest stubborn behaviors when they are being taught discipline. If we as parents show negligence in the upbringing of our children in the way God commands, we will be faced with shame, disappointment and sorrow, for parents who do foolish things, also foolish children bring grief to their fathers and bitter regrets to their mothers.

Parents have to go to God in prayer to entrust and conserve their children, because of the many dangers to which they are exposed to and how the world and the devil persecutes them, by trying to destroy their dignity as children of God and to cast them in the filth of sin.

Selected Scriptures

- Genesis 8:21b

Notes

Chapter 4

CHILDREN

Some time ago a grandmother was heard saying that she wished she had her grandchildren before her own children. This is because she was enjoying the time of her life with her grandchildren which she did not have with her own.

Precious little ones, how sweet they can be, and of course we all know that they are special gifts form God. For a moment, just think about children in Iraq and other parts of the world, misplaced, abandoned and left to fend for themselves, just because of world conflicts.

Children have no quarrels with governments or parents, yet some of them have to endure hardships and suffering for no actions of their own. They should not be made to suffer in any way, manner or form, for they did not ask to come here. However, now that they are here it is the responsibilities of grown ups to see them through the rough spots of life journey.

Since the subject of parenting from a biblical perspective is being discussed, it is fitting to remind parents of the awesome responsibilities that lie on their shoulders. Jesus did not have children of his own and as you are aware He loved them dearly, so then how should we treat our children?

C. Create in them a desire for God. Mark 10:13-16

As parent we are called to be teachers, the ultimate goal of Christian parenting is not children who merely have knowledge about God. It is children who have a personal relationship with God. It is children who really believe that God's Words are relevant in every aspect of their lives. This involves teaching our children the ways of the Lord, helping them to understand the characters of God, helping them to understand the darkness of their own hearts and the danger of walking alone while trusting in themselves. Teach them to lean on the righteous One. Teach them to Keep God's Word in their hearts because we are living in perilous times. The enemy is out there lying in wait, but if they have the savior within, nothing can separate them from the love of God.

H. Hold them in Prayer. I Samuel 1:27-28.

Pray for them and with them. Do not curse them; did you know that the Jewish people designed worship service for their children? They devote religious prayer service at home with their children, the results are, they are very successful and prosperous in what they do, that is why we have to go to them for employment. Bless your children instead of cursing them. Pray for them in Jesus name. Pray for them faithfully and consistently. Pray for them according to God's will, pray for them in the mornings, evenings and at nights. Our secret weapons must be our prayers. So what are we to pray for?

1. That God will keep them pure.
2. That they may be delivered from the evil ones.
3. That God's law may remain in their hearts.
4. That their peace may be great

5. They will learn to discern good from evil.
6. They may choose companions who are wise, not fools and immoral.

I. Instruct them in the Word of God. Deut.6:4-9

From the beginning of time God intended the family to be the basic unit for society. If we fail to instruct them, then who will? The schools? You got to be kidding. Thanks be to God for Christians schools, the ones that remain faithful in teaching biblical morals and values. The government schools are not in the business of teaching biblical values, in fact they can't even read the Bible much less to pray. The people in the streets want to corrupt their minds because they are vulnerable and are easily led. We have a responsibility to train them right, listen, when you do as you are required to do and they go astray, the burden of guilt is not on you, they just make the wrong choice. Remember God gives us free wills, people have choices. You did not fail, they did.

L. Lead them in the path of Righteousness. Gen.18:19

Teach them to depend on God. Give us this day our daily bread. In the Wilderness the people of Israel learned to depend upon the Lord for their daily food. Sometimes you will have to say no to them, but no does not mean never, sometimes it means later which is always greater. God was silent in respect to Jesus while He was on the cross, and it was good after all. We are now children of God with a bright future. Thanks be to God for saying no at times, after all He is God, He knows best.

D. Devise plan for their lives

Know your children's needs. Today's children need guidelines and guard lines more than ever. They also need shepherds who understand the times and their hearts. It should be made clear that children understand that there are three 8 hours work shifts in a given day, therefore, they need to choose one.

R. Responsibility.

Teach them to be responsible and that actions have consequences. You have no control over the consequences but you can control your actions. Teach them to respect the rights of others. Teach them to respect people's properties. Teach them to speak the truth at all times, no matter the consequences. As it is said of old, "Speak the truth and speak it ever, cause it what it will, he who hides the wrong he did does the wrong things still." Teach them the value of life, "thou shall not kill" it is a Commandment. Teach them that wrongs are always wrong. Teach them that hatred is not of God, but love covered all sins.

E. Entreat Them.

Entreat means to beseech or implore. All things pertaining to God is absolute, they are not debatable. What joy it would be if more families take this approach. Take them to Sunday school and Bible study. If you think education is expensive wait until you see the price of ignorance. Remember whatsoever you sow that shall you also reap. A word to the wise is sufficient.

N. Nurture them. Eph. 6:4

God has called us to lead, guide, nurture, correct and discipline our children. God has placed us with authority over our children and we must be willing to assume that responsibility. Nurturing a child means to give them a well rounded and stable environment. Teach them how to sit, how to stand, how to walk, how to enter a conversation and how to stop a quarrel. Let them be aware of their mistakes and correct them with love. Teach them how to love, how to give, how to receive and be appreciative. Teach them how to become a well mannered citizen. The end result is they will remember and love you for your nurturing.

Selected Scriptures

- Mark 10:13-16
- I Samuel 1:27-28
- Deuteronomy 6:4-9
- Genesis 18:19
- Ephesians 6:4

Notes

Chapter 5

Children are Gifts.

"Behold children are a gift of the Lord, the fruit of the womb is a reward." **Ps. 127: 3**

Gifts are given in appreciation for something done by someone; they are cherished and appreciated because they were rewarded for good deeds.

In the case of God's precious gifts, children, we are to be more appreciative because they comes from God. All good gifts come from the Lord. Parents are therefore, responsible to cherish and care for their precious gifts. God will hold us responsible for His gifts. What is a man's purpose of accumulating wealth? What is the purpose of building dynasty if there are no children to hold it after him? Remember the great Napoleon; he could not create a dynasty, because he had no children. Hundreds of wealthy people would give a lot if they could have children around them. Children are a heritage, which God himself must give, or a man will die childless and thus his house will be unbuilt. God gives children as gifts, not as penalty or burden. They are a token of good if a man knows how to receive and treat them.

There should be no reason why you should be apprehensive for your families, there should be no reason why you should be worrying yourself with such great restlessness and labor, God will take care of you and your children, since they are his precious gifts. Has it ever occur to you that there is much reason why the poor has a great number of children, no land, no properties but a lot of children. To many He gave silver and gold and a womb that beareth not, to other He gave children.

Children are God's Gift to Parents.
- Genesis 33:5. "And he lifted up his eyes, and saw the woman and the children; and said, who are those with thee? And he said. The children which **God hath graciously given** thy servant."
- Genesis 48:9. "They are my sons, whom **God hath given me** in this place."
- Joshua 24:3. "I took your father Abraham… and multiplied his seed, and **gave him Isaac**."
- Ruth 4:13b. "The **Lord gave her conception**, and she bares a son."
- Psalm 127:3, "Fatherhood itself is the **Lord's Gift**, the fruit womb is a reward that **comes from God.**"
- Isaiah 8:18. "Behold, I and the **children whom the Lord hath given me** are for signs and wonders in Israel **from the Lord of host**, which dwells in mount Zion."

How then should we receive these gifts?

It is evident from Scriptures that children are gifts from God. How then shall we receive these precious gifts? We have two choices here, reject a or accept it. Since these gifts are God given, one would be wise to accept them gracefully.

Matthew 18:5 says, "Whosoever shall receive one such little child in my name receives Me." The word 'receive' that is used here is the Greek word, 'dechomal' which means to accept a gift readily and heartily. In essence when we receive a little child we are actually receiving Jesus Himself. So to welcome a baby is to welcome Jesus. Let us receive our children whole heartedly and with positive attitudes.

Why God does give us Children?
- **To procreate the earth**. Gen. 1:28
- **To Honor us.** I Chronicles 25:4-6. God honored Heman with fourteen (14) sons and three daughters. He was exalted and given power for his greater joy. God has not given children to us to degrade us but as a blessing and honor for our greater joy especially in our old age. The more godly children we have, the more power we have for God in the earth. The more power we have over the enemy. The world may look on those with a large family as inferior. But this is far from the truth; this deception is used by the enemy who is the Deceiver and a Liar.
- **To do us Good.** Deuteronomy 30:5. "He will do thee good, and multiply thee." When God wants to do something good for us, He gives us children.
- **To give us Joy.** Luke 1:14ff. "And you will have joy and gladness, and many will rejoice at his birth." God gives us children to bring us great joy. Godly children bring much joy to the family. The older you get and the more mature you become you will realize that material things perish after a period of time but children are lasting gifts that will keep you forever.
- **To defend us.** Psalm 127:5. The man who has his quiver full of them shall not be ashamed. They are the weapons when the enemies come to his gates. He will have children to stand up for him.
- **To care for us.** Proverbs 23:22: Isaiah 58:7, Matthew 15:4-8 and I Timothy 5:3-16. As you will see, there are many Scriptures related to this subject. It is all in God's plan for the new generation to care for the older ones. Failing this, the whole nation will be affected.

Selected Scriptures

- Psalm 127:3,5
- Genesis 1:28, 33:5
- Genesis 48:9
- Joshua 24:3
- Ruth 4:13b
- Isaiah 8:18, 58:7
- Matthew 15:4-8,18:5
- I Chronicles 25:4-5
- Deuteronomy 30:5
- Luke 1:14ff
- Proverbs 23:22
- I Timothy 5:3-16

Chapter 6

Teach Them Good Manners

Etiquette should not be practice for special occasions, but must be a way of life taught by all parent. In doing so Jesus' advise to "do unto others as you would like them do to you" will be practiced. How then can parents teach their children good manners? I'm glad you ask!

- Children are progressive works. Realize that children are children not adults; they are in the learning process, most of the times they do not know appropriate behavior. Do not be embarrassed when they make mistakes. You should only be embarrassed if you fail to teach them good behavior.
- Fill you home with love. Show children the kind of love you want them to embrace themselves. Love that is unconditional, sacrificial and focused. Make it your duty to let children know that you love them. Accept them for who they are even when they are wrong.
- Teach them to be respectful to others. Teach them the sanctity of life, human beings and animals have values and should be treated as such. Live a life patterned off integrity so that you

will be personally worthy of your children's respect. Teach them to address adults with titles and or last names. Mr. Brown, Mrs. Brown, Dr. Do-good etc). Teach them to give respect to their seniors at all times, to be polite, offer seats to them, stand up when they are being introduced, respond when spoken to and for heaven sake teach them to say thank you, No sir, No Mom etc. Encourage them to repeat task over and over until they get it right. Remind them not to use disrespectful words or a rude tone of voice. And model behaviors for them in your own lives.

Teach them respect by listening when they speak, allowing them to make age- appropriate choices, never demeaning or embarrassing them, being considerate of their needs, validating their feelings, allowing them to have personal space and things, understanding their emotions and giving them permission to voice personal opinions and concerns. Teach them to respect their siblings by prohibiting name calling, fighting and property destruction.

- Teach them the magic words. You would be surprise how many children do not bother to say "thank you" for things given or done to them. Never let it be said that you fail to teach them the magic words, Words, like, "Please," "Thank you," "excuse me," "You're welcome," "and I'm sorry". Explain when, why and how to use these words and the importance of using them.
- Teach them to be of Good Behavior in public. Have you ever gone to the supermarket and observed the behavior of some children? Sad indeed, I know! Most times they were not taught to behave in public. They should be taught not to, run indoors, use loud voices, talk while someone is speaking to them, cut in line, chew gums loudly and bring phones to church.
- Teach them basic hygiene by taking at lease a daily bath or shower, wash their hands prior to meals, and brush their teeth each morning and evening.

- Teach them good table Manners. This aught to be on your priority list, to eat meals together at dinner tables as a family aught to and to sit properly.
- Teach them to set the dinner table for formal and informal meal settings.
- Teach them to sit quietly, to chew with their mouths closed, placed napkins on their laps, and keep their elbows off the table.
- Teach them to say grace for their meals by giving thanks to God's for His daily provisions.
- Teach them to make and keep wholesome friends.
- Teach them to be loyal, encouraging, respectful and thoughtful of others.
- Teach them to treat others the same way how they would like to be treated, like boys holding doors and pull out chairs for girls and treat members of the opposite sex with respect.

Notes

Chapter 7

Open line Communications

Every parent of a teenager is anxious to build a strong line of communication with their teens. But sadly, the opposite is most often true. As our children transform into adolescence, it is absolutely necessary that one adapt the style of communication to the changes taking place in our children. What was no-hormonal now becomes laced with hormones. Total dependence shift gears up to independence.

According to the Gospel of Matthew, Jesus says, *"come to me all who are heavy laden* (the condition of teen), *and I will give you rest"* (the parent's part) Matt.11:28

This passage depicts the metaphorical conditions of the teenagers and the "should be role" of the parents with the hope that we as parent are rest for our children. Too many times parents become a burden and hardship to their children. Moms have the tendency to do the "Energizer" communication that just keep on going and dads have the tendency to tune out when communication is most needed.

To achieve an objective balance, it is important for us as parents to transition with our children and to change the style of communication. If we can do this successfully, then the day when our children begin to struggle or have difficulties and desperately need someone to talk to.... We are the ones they will turn to.

Do not stay there and wonder what is the opportune time to start building the line of communication. It is right Now, before the struggle, hardship and difficulties start. And never stop working at that when there is a conflict, remember this is progressive.

Now, here are a few lessons for building the bridge of communications. Start by laying a few rules, not the ones to confuse or dictate but to adapt and embrace.
- Fun filled activities. Plan game's night, like Friday nights, play games together, laugh, and no spiritual lesson attached, just pure fun.
- Peer day. On Saturdays mother takes daughter shopping while father takes son to work or ball games.
- Create a sense of wonder. Instead of always telling children the answers, leave them with a question. Remembering that not all questions have immediate answers, by this they will learn to think independently.
- Wait to be invited. People have a way of offering opinions, (Scripture says that a fool delights in airing his own opinion). Silence will provoke questions like, so what do you think? And what would you do, etc.
- Consider others to be more important. This is easier said than done, however, we have the tendency to always put our children first, this will affect the way you discipline them, the way you treat them, and the way you show them grace when you are disappointed and upset.

Parents are challenge today to commit to building bridges of communication with your children. Make time to communicate to them and to know them no matter the strain and hardship sometimes. There is always HOPE and God is watching.

Selected Scriptures

- Matthew 11:28

Notes

Chapter 8

Discipline and Sparing the Rod.

Love your children, you aught to, therefore you will correct them (Proverbs 22: 15) "Foolishness is bound in the heart of a child; but the rod of correction shall drive them far from him" lack of love for children prevents parents taking the right direction in discipline. Don't get me wrong, the Scripture does not approve or encourage child abuse. The rod of correction has proven effective when administered in love. A child's pain causes parents to suffer as well. When love is shown to the child, his soul is alive in the hearts of parents. If we discipline with anger, our children will not accomplish good results because confidence between children and parents will be broken.

Proverbs 13:24 states as follows, "he that spareth his rod hateth his son; but he that loveth him chaseneth him be-times", in a culture like ours we think a "good beating" (whipping) does the child good. Remember parenting does not come with guidelines. Discipline your children carefully. Think before you act; never discipline your children when you are angry or upset. Give yourself time to calm down. Children live what they learn, how you discipline your child is a way of teaching them.

If you discipline them with violence then they may think that forms of violence are always the way of resolving conflicts. This writer does not believe that whipping a child mercilessly is a justifiable act of discipline, this is known as violence to the extend where you are qualified as a terrorist, the end result is fear not love.

Mothers and fathers should develop Christian habits of prayer, the practice of good deeds and a spirit of sacrifice in us will enhance our Christian attitudes of fraternal charity and mutual forgiveness. What you teach your children is like a grain of sand on the beach. Remember other people will have influence on them too.

Our homes should be fashioning them to approach their new frontier with strength and determination. God knows what lies ahead, you don't. Let your voice be heard far off in the wilderness, but no matter how small it is, you will be heard, because you have done your Godly part. The challenge now is what we can do for our children. The best of anything comes from hard work, dedication and humility, and this should be a reminder to all parents.

The greater joy is not only teaching but sharing with your children the throes of life that comes our way. In the final analysis our diversity at the beginning has not been divisive. We are to remember that God will conduct our affairs in accordance with His perfect will.

Selected Scriptures

- Proverbs 13: 24 & 22:15:

Notes

Chapter 9

God's Purpose for Marriage

Long before God established the Church, the state, and the schools, he created marriage. The goal for this God ordained institution is clearly set out in Genesis 2:21, Matthew 19:6 and Mark 10:8.

Oneness is God's purpose for marriage. Yet most of us have only dimly perceived the supreme goal God intends for a husband and a wife to achieve. In essence, most couples do not have a concept of what they are trying to accomplish in their marriage.

The oneness designed for marriage partners is compared to the relationship believers shared with Christ. In this "mystical union" Christ, the bridegroom, joins Himself to His bride, the Church: and they become one. In this union with Christ, man enjoys his highest spiritual communion. On earth, God intends for us to enjoy a similar union in marriage. Ephesians 5:23-33.

To understand God's original purpose for marriage, we must go back to the Garden of Eden. God placed Adam in a perfect environment and provided for his every possible need. Anything he desired was available to him for the taking; he simply had to pick it off the tree. This man whom God created was the epitome of humanity-physically perfect with a superior intellect.

Yet, when God looked upon Adam, with his tremendous mental capacities, his physical prowess, his perfect environment, and his spiritual communication with the creator, He found man lacking. God said, "It is not good that man should be alone". (Gen.2:18)

Many groups in the world today say, "God, You are wrong," it is good for man to be alone. It is truly exciting. Even married people accept the notion of modern society and go their separate way, never realizing that the deepest, most fulfilling spiritual union that can be experienced with another human being is found in marriage. (of the opposite sex of course)

Although Adam enjoyed the companion of the beautiful animals, he did not have a suitable helper. None of the animals could meet Adam's needs, so the Creator designed a completely new being for Adam. God put Adam to sleep, took one of his ribs, and out of this rib built a woman. Adam responded by "she is bone of my own bone and flesh, Her name is "Woman" because she was taken out of man" (Gen.2:23).

When a man and a woman gets married they are not two but one, even though they are not from the same body like Adam and Eve were, there is still a unique oneness between them that no other human relationship can enjoy. Husbands, your wife is you, wives, your husband is you. If you can grasp this fact hold on to it, your marriage will never be the same again.

Married couples need to commit themselves to the fulfillment of their vows on their wedding day. The Bible says it is a grievous and heinous sin to break a vow, and God is greatly displeased with those who do so." When you make vow to God, do not delay in fulfilling it, He has no pleasure in fools: fulfill your vow" (Eccl. 5:4).

We need to have this same attitude toward our marriage vows. Divorce is not a viable option to marital problems. Commit yourself to the permanence of your marriage, and don't even mention the word divorce in your home.

This is built on commitment "for better or worse". In sickness an in health. When you get married you commit yourself for life to one another, there should not be a footnote in the back of your mind in case things get really tough one will check out.

Husbands and wives who do not see their marriage as an irrevocable, indissoluble, and permanent union will never experience the oneness that Christ says exists in that special relationship. You may be thinking that this means you are condemned to a life – sentence of misery and heartache. "Oh, he will never change! He is just like his father." Or, "she'll never be any different; she is just like her mother."

Remember, the whole thrust of biblical message is that God can change people. So if you take those negative positions, you are insulting God and his Words. By the power of the Holy Spirit, your spouse can become the husband or wife God wants them to be.

God has a plan for improving your relationship, if you commit to His Words. If you commit yourself to discovering how you can implement His perfect will for you, you will be successful.

How is the oneness in your marriage? Do you have two soloists, or do you have a duet? Do you have your own interest, your own friends, your own enjoyment, and your own entertainment? Do you allow the world to pull you apart? Do the two of you go your own ways and occasionally meet at the home refueling center?, if these describe your marriage, then ask God to help you experience the deeper joy, love and peace that come with true oneness.

Selected Scriptures

- Genesis 2:18,21,23
- Matthew 19:6
- Mark 10:18
- Ephesians 5:23-33
- Ecclesiastes 5:4

Notes

Chapter 10

Divorce.

Deut.24:1-4
Matt.5:19-21

The Bible states emphatically that the Lord hates divorce; therefore, at what level should divorce be acknowledged?

Moses states that "when a man hath taken a wife, and marries her, and it came to pass that she find no favor in his eyes, because he hath found some uncleanness in her; then let him write her a bill of divorcement, and give it in her hand, and send her out of his house". (Deut.24:10), please note that the reason for this divorce was sexual sin, because the penalty for sexual sin is death by stoning. (Lev.20:10ff).

So that was the Old Testament account, the New Testament referred to the OT in Matthew 5.

Consequences of divorce.
- Children are affected when there is a divorce in any union. Emotionally and financially.

  The decision of custody must come to mind, who is the right person to be granted custody of the children, it is said that the mother should care for the girls if she is mentally capable of doing so, then what happen to the father and daughter relationship? While on the other hand boys are better cared for by the father for manhood development, then what happen to the mother and son relationship?

- **It is a physical experience.**

  It may seems to be a good thing that ever happen to you at first, but later on you will find out that it is not as easy as you had envision. In most cases divorces never work out the way it was planned. Life after divorce is always changing and you will not have a lot of control over those changes. We often get hopelessly caught up in parenting plans when we first separate, and, while that is important, it doesn't usually prepare you for the ongoing changes, challenges, and negotiations that go on for years, changes that you don't always like but learn to live with. There is the ongoing tradeoff of deciding which battles will catch your children in the middle, and figuring out when one must learn to lose the battle to win the war. A child needs peace of mind. Life takes twists and turns that was never in the plan, so you must learn to go with the flow or be hopelessly mired in your own anger or disappointment.

- Favored Parent. Remember when your kids asked you who you loved the best, you knew what a silly (but honest) question it was because everyone likes being the first at heart of those they love. Unfortunately in a divorce, when parents aren't together to hear news in a shared situation, your child will tell one before the other. It doesn't mean you're the less favored, secondary or unflavored parent, but it sure does feel like it. So you have to learn to forgive yourself when those competitive feelings crop up from the dark depth of your soul and learn to laugh at them.

Effects of Divorce.

Countless scholars have conducted studies on the effects of divorce on children, it is determined that this have both short and long term terms. While some mental health professionals believe that a divorce is more traumatic at some age than others, there is certainly no good time for a young person to endure the divorce of parents. Children will and may respond in diverse ways and manners when they learn of the pending divorce of their parents including denial, shame, anger, and depression.

- **Denial.** A common attitude most often displayed is denial. Some children may respond to their parents' divorce by acting as if it isn't happening or by insisting to themselves that their parents won't even go through with it. This form of denial can be devastating in that, it becomes internal problems which sometimes never heal.
- **Shame.** Shame and embarrassment are very common responses to parents' divorce. Many are so ashamed that they refused to inform their closest friends. Many children feels guilty that their family is in turmoil and cannot be reconciled. As such they feel a certain degree of responsibility for their parents' actions. The immediate and sudden change in their lives can be devastating mainly because of the change in lifestyle.
- **Anger.** Children cannot be blame for feeling a sense of anger on the news of parents' divorce after all, this will certainly disrupts their lives and environments for reasons they don't even understand. They feel a sense of abandonment upon separation from the party they may love more dearly than the other. Children are very sensitive where family life is concern; they believe that father and mother should always be together in one happy family.
- **Depression.** Depression is a prolonged form of sadness normally associated with the following, apathy, loss of appetite, hopelessness, withdrawal, and loss of ability to play. Such depression can last for a long period of time and is bound to affect their abilities. While a certain degree of depression is

natural and understandable among many children of divorce parents, long-term depression is not at all healthy.

Teenagers may also experience others emotional long-term effects like, academic problems, substance abuse, sexual activity and suicidal threats.

Advice for divorce. Try to avoid it at all cost. Parents must be committed to prayers and quality family time.

Selected Scripture

- Deuteronomy 24:1-4
- Leviticus 20:10ff
- Matthew 5:19-21

Notes

Chapter 11

Co-parental Relationship

As a Christian, it is my awesome duty to encouraged married couples to do all within their powers to stay to together for the benefit of their own wellbeing as well as for the children. Studies have shown that the quality of father-child relationships inside and outside of marriage is strongly correlated with the quality of the co-parental relationship than is true for the just single parent[2]. (Belsky & Volling, 1987: Cox, Owen, Lewis & Henderson, 1989. Fathers appear to withdraw from their child when they are not getting along with the mothers, whereas mothers do not show a similar level of withdrawal. This is one way to understand the tendency of fathers to remove themselves from their children's lives after a breakup with the mother, especially if they have a negative relationship with the mother[3].(Ahrons & Miller), 1993)

---

[2] Belsky.J. & Volling, B.L. Mothering, Fathering and marital interaction in the family triad during infancy.

[3] Ahrons, C.R. & Miller, R.B.1993.The effect of the post divorce relationship. American Journal of Orthopsychiatry, Pp 63, 441-450.

According to the authors Furstenberg and Cherlin (1991) they have asserted, for many men, marriage and parenthood are a "package deal." [4] or one might say that in American culture, a woman is a mother all of her life, but a man is a father if he has a wife. Furthermore, if he has a wife but does not get along with her, he may be present as a father, but the quality if his relationship with his children is apt to suffer.

This writer is cognizant of the fact that at times it is difficult to get along peacefully especially for young couples. This is more prevalent in the absence of pre-marital counseling for young and first time married couples. It is difficult for two strangers coming from different cultures to come together and dwell together without differences of opinions, but for the benefit of the child/children our differences must be dealt with as soon as possible in an amicable manner.

One of the reasons that fathering is particularly sensitive to the marital or co-parental relationship is that standards and expectations for fathering appear to be more variable than that of mothering. The demands are great for fathers, especially when boys are in the union. Who is better equipped to train the boys than their fathers? You're right again, their father.

Christians advocate and fully support the marriage of parents, while some may argue that being married is not important, because cohabiting couples are capable of good parenting, and this may be true, but what kind of example are you setting for the children?

The Christian principles are conclusive, and in general practice both morally and ethically the kind of mother-father relationship that must be conducive to responsible parenting which fosters a caring, committed, and loving environment is found in marriage.

---

[4] Furstenberg, F.F. 1985. Parenting Apart; Journal of Marriage and the Family. 47, 893-904.

Chapter 12

Fathers

I am fortunate, my father is a Christian, and he was married to my mother until she passed away when I was only two years old. That terrible motor vehicle accident on Spur Tree Hill in Manchester, Jamaica in 1960., which claimed the life of my dear mother along with others. How cruel life can be at times.

His name is on my birth certificate, he still continues to be of constant presence and influence in my life.
- He taught me how to pray, he taught by example and precept to respect everyone irrespective of their class or status.
- He taught me that we are all God's children.
- He taught me the ways of a righteous man, yes, I am fortunate. As a consequence I have grown up with a multi-faceted concept of manhood and fatherhood, which goes far beyond the stereotypical macho stud.

As one of eight children (six boys and two girls) in my home, my father was the ideal leader in this family; he never takes a day off much less a vacation, because he understood the importance of fatherhood.

Today he had already celebrated his 80th birth date, with all of his children grown; he is still going like an energized full charged battery. He never stops. This is one of the reasons why he is my role model.

There are many different circumstances that caused fathers to be absent from homes.

While some are unavoidable others are not. He was aware that he was bringing up someone else's future husbands or wives, mothers or fathers. His attitudes instilled in us from childhood are the building blocks for our adult lives. As I went down the list of values and related these to my own children it finally occurred to me how fortunate my other siblings and I were to inherit so rich a legacy.

As a boy, the first male figure I saw was my father, by nurturing his boys he was teaching us to value our own masculinity. This man was available and enjoys being the man who gives us a healthy sexual role model to follow.

My father also knew the importance of paternal nurturance for his daughters, this is necessary to their enjoying being the women they are today. Fathers give daughters their first experiences relating to the opposite sex. When father is out of the loop, passive, non-nurturing, uninvolved family life, the daughter misses out on early lessons about balanced male-female relationships. The result is, many fall into risky and uncomfortable relationships rather than healthy and comfortable ones. My father was a model and his children did not have to look further than home for a role model, he was right there.

Dad was a good provider, he is aware that being a good provider is crucial to his masculinity and feelings about himself as a father. This accounts for some long hours he spent away from home. However, he never compromises his fathering with his work.

Very often he would take us to work with him in order to see the awesome responsibility he carried and to demonstrate the importance of work. As such, all of his children benefited early in life from working. Not only did we understand his work habits but we accept his absence from home willfully and justifiably.

There is one very important thing I wish to mention about my father, as I have already mentioned; my mother died tragically when I was two years old. Between the ages of two and ten years old, as far as I can recall, my father never, I mean never, absolutely never take another woman in our home until he was joined in holy matrimony with his new bride the former Ms.Gladys Martin.(Now deceased). Now this man needs some credit and adoration for his morals. He was aware of the need to set good examples for his children. He also understood the implications that his behavior would have on us.

Thanks be to God for fathers like him, God fearing, ethically moral, sincere, loving, kind, and gentle but firm.

This world would do a lot better with more fathers like him.

Notes

Chapter 13

Boys to Men.

From time to time churches have been recognizing the need to have specific programs and ministries targeting young men in and out of church.

This is a very healthy development, for as the church succeeds, it will in some way stem the downward spiral of negative male behavior among boys and men often manifested in increased violent crime and poor grades in primary through tertiary institutions.

Many do not accept the argument that violent crime is largely induced by poverty and an under-performing economy. The ever-escalating crimes in the book of many are directly linked or related to fatherlessness- i.e. the underperformance of fathers in investing in the lives of their sons with moral and spiritual capital needed for responsible adolescent and manhood.

Fathers are entrusted and given the responsibility to train their sons. Failing this, very soon many of them will be trained by the "Dons" and other "Thugs."

Many boys are over- mothered and under- fathered. I believe wholeheartedly, that God wired men to father and He wired women to mother.

The problem is that often the man won't take his fatherhood serious enough thereby causing the woman to do the mothering and try to father something she was not created to do.

We cannot deny the fact that a lot of children turned out well when mommy was the only one there to mother and "father" them. Just think how much better they would have maximize their potential had they have daddy there taking fatherhood seriously.

This writer believes that every son needs from his father: vision, direction, and solid answers to such questions as what is man's responsibility. What does a man believe? How does a man believe? What should a man try to achieve?

Robert Lewis, in his book" Raising a Modern-Day Knight", uses the medieval knighthood as his model for raising boys. He argues that the knights were the Promise-Keepers of that era-embodying well–defined masculine ideals, and clear rites of passage.[5]

Knighthood he continues, involved rigorous training beginning at a page, (puberty) to squire (late teens) to knight (early adulthood). "From page to squire to knight, a young man could envision the process, count the cost and pursue his dreams.[6]

---

[5] Robert Lewis. Raising A Modern- Day Knight. Pp.45-105 1954

[6] Pp. 107-127

Sadly, for a boy today, there is no equivalent path on the journey to manhood. There are no landmark, no milestone and no legend to guide a boy on his journey and no ceremonies to tell him when manhood begins. With all the discussions and debates today on the subject of manhood, there remains great void.

A godly man is someone who rejects passivity, accepts responsibility, lead courageously and expects great rewards. This man tries to be like Jesus, when He was tempted, He firmly stood his grounds and rebuked the devil. Unlike Adam, who blamed the woman for his sins, he should have at least defeat the serpent by firmly rebuke it and drive it out of the garden, after all he was in charge.

This is what we are seeing in our homes today, fathers blaming mothers, mothers blaming someone or something else, and the end result is a fatherless home. This is now called dysfunctional homes.

Conventional portrait of fatherhood are not always wrong but incomplete when these portraits do not address "a transcendent cause," conventional manhood emphasizes the pursuit of "position"; being highly competitive to achieve "success" (even if this means not giving due attention to family life) and the obsession with acquiring power, wealth and influence.

Some fathers are danger to their sons; they fail to see how much emotional capital God had given them to train their sons. In the formative years of a boy's life, his dad is a hero, a kind of superman. That is the opportune time for dads to make a lasting and convincing imprint on the boy's life. The Bible says it well, "the glory of children are theirs fathers". (Proverbs 17:6b)

We will never have a better society until fathers invest morality and spirituality in their sons. A healthy and vibrant masculinity goes hand-in-hand with social stability.

Selected Scriptures

- Proverbs 17:6b

Chapter 14

Father's Day

In the eyes of God every day is Father's day, this writer has never taken time off from being a father but society assigned a day to celebrate father's day.

A day consigned to the paying of homage to the fathers among us. This celebration stands contrast to Mothers Day, which is traditionally replete with emotionally charged private and public tributes to ours mothers, the stalwarts and backbone of society.

To a great many, Father's day is devoid of significance as there is no father to receive the thanks, praise and well wishes. To others it serves as a painful reminder of unfulfilled aspirations and barren dreams. To some it serves as a purely perfunctory exercise meant to appease undeserving fathers jealous of the accolades heaped upon mothers; and to the few it is a day filled with warmth, strengthened and renewed bonds that serve to form character.

Society has become permeated with indiscipline, disrespect and violence. Many search in vain for the answer to ills within the society. In despair we seek to remedy the fruit of our affliction (crime/corruption/violence) and overlook the root cause. The basic family structure lacks the balance so necessary for the proper environment, in which we raise our children.

The natural order of things requires the strong stabilizing and disciplinary male influence in order that children may grow properly rounded. Wayward fathers have cheated their children our of a complete character development. They have weakened the very family infrastructure on which our society is built and set the stage for the inevitable implosion of values and morality.

We need to send a message to deadbeat dads; we need to enforce the laws governing parental responsibilities and obligations. We need to encourage fathers to participate in every aspect of family life so that society may once more achieve the balance and harmony that are so sadly lacking.

Chapter 15

The Joy of being a Godly Dad

The greatest joys of my life have come from being married to my wife. We hold the record for having the longest honeymoon in the world, it is still going on and we have pledge before God and man to continue. Whenever I look at her, I still tingle inside. She has been my joy (ironically her middle name is Joy) and inspiration ever since we met.

This wonder woman, my wife, has blessed me with two wonderful children. Being apart of this wonderful family has given me identity, support, inspiration and clarity of purpose and they make sure I keep my priorities straight.

My wife and I are very driven; we come from the old school. We were taught that if you were going to compete in this world, you have to run faster and harder than others. We did and continue to do just that. We were also taught to put God and family first. We have spent our lives together trying to balance our community involvement, career and family. We have always fought to protect our family and our sacred family time.

We worshipped together and always spent quality time one night per week as family night. Family time is time we do home worship.

On Sundays I take the children to Sunday school, as I am a Sunday school teacher, my wife would joined us later for morning worship service.

Recently our little son, DeSean, celebrated his ninth birthday. I try to take him to church every opportunity I get. As we celebrated DeSean's birthday, I realized that the greatest gift we could have been given him was sitting right infront of us. The greatest gift God can give a couple is children. When you look at your children today or tonight, look them straight in the eyes and say, "you are the greatest and most precious gift God could give and I thank God for you".(Psalm 127:3)

I recently spent a day with my son, just him and me. We were children again. We ate junk food, laughed and acted crazy and enjoyed each other. I am an ardent fan of the Atlanta Braves Baseball team; my son is a Basketball fan, when the Braves lost a game he mourns with me. He felt my pain that my team went down in defeat. He was amazed that I was not upset. In their losses I found my victory, victory for me was that he was with me spending quality time with a wonderful boy.

Sometimes, as parents, we are so busy that we forget to guide and raise our children. We forget to spend quality time with them, we do not take time to look at them and say "Thank God for you,

Parenting from a Christian Perspective

thank God for giving us wonderful children". Have you thank God for your children lately?

This writer is convinced that fathers now comes in different packages, below is a list of diverse ways.
- Some children have fathers who live far away and send them money or clothing.
- Some children have fathers who live nearby and visit regularly.
- Some children have fathers that raise them alone.
- Others have fathers who share home and caring duties with their mothers.
- Others have fathers who look after them all the time, so that mothers can work.
- Some children have fathers they stay with at weekends and on the Holidays.
- Others have fathers who are in jail.
- Some children have fathers who live at home, but are rarely there.
- Others have foster fathers or step fathers.
- Some children have fathers that are too poor to provide for them.
- Some have an uncle or grandfather who fathers them.
- And some children have no father figure.
- There are some fathers that read bedtime stories to their children.
- And there are fathers who cannot read.
- There are fathers who love and care for their children.
- And there are fathers that neglect and abuse their children.
- Some fathers attend the birth and every event in their children's lives.
- Others have never even met their children.
- Some fathers are ill, some commit crimes and some abuse their children's mothers.
- Some are confident in their parenting role and take great pride in it .
- And others are frightened of these responsibilities.
- Some fathers run away from their children.

- And others, desperate to see them, and are prevented from doing so.

Fatherhood is different in so many ways for so many children, but one thing is universal, what fathers do....**Matters to Children.**[7]

This reflection challenges us to get away from the shallow thinking and mindless stereotypes about fathers and their relationship with their children. At the end of the day fathers should be able to say without a shadow of a doubt, "I have done all within my powers to provide and protect all my children," Based upon my understanding of fatherhood, it brings delight to God when we take care of our children, as such it also brings joy in our lives of being great dads.

---

[7] Barker Gary Dr. and Janet Brown. Head of the Caribbean Child Development Center.

Selected Scriptures

- Psalm 127:3

Notes

Chapter 16

Responsibilities of mothers to Daughters

So far the burning issues regarding the important responsibilities and relationships between fathers and sons have been discussed. It is not that mothers to daughters' relationship have been neglected, but since it would appears that we are loosing our young men at a rapid speed it was fitting that it be dealt with early. With that said, the time has come to look at the relationships and responsibilities of mothers to their daughters. The following are two of the most valuable principles women should teach their daughters, which will be discussed in this order, 1) Modesty and 2) Responsibility to their husbands.

1. Modesty.

> 1 Timothy 2:9-10. *In likewise manner also, that women adorn themselves in modest apparel, with shame facedness and sobriety; not to dress with braided hair, or gold, or pearls, or costly array; but (with becometh women professing godliness)with good works.*

In short this means "proper clothing," respectable and honorable apparel reflects a godly woman inner life. Modest dressing was encouraged for our women not only in churches but in general appearances.

Standing in the teller line at the bank, I noticed that all the bank patrons were getting agitated at the slow pace of service. Then she walked in, a long legged young lady in high heels and very skimpily dressed, I mean you could see almost every thing that I was not supposed to see in a public place. As she scanted across the bank's lobby floor I sensed that everyone was holding their breath in awe wondering why any sensible human being could leave their home in this manner. Onlookers were turning their heads back and forth at each other, then at the woman and again at each other.

The first thing that came to my mind is everybody's curiosity and what the Bible warns about women like that. The incident happened years ago, but it's no laughing matter today as we often see young women dressed more like stereotypical hookers than modest young women.

Now, whatever baits that you are using will determine the type of fish you will catch, if a young woman dresses seductively guys are likely to treat her as if she wanted to be seduced. She is going to get attention from lustful guys who just want to have fun and not godly ones who want to guard themselves against sexual immorality.

If we want our young ladies to be treated with dignity and respect which they deserve, we will have to start setting the high standard of modesty and to teach them to dress modestly. If we want to protect them from the roaming wolves who are only interesting in their bodies rather than their minds, heart and spirit, we will have to teach them how to shop for clothes that represent a passion for purity rather than a plea for attention and invitation.

On one occasion, this writer spoke with a parent about the manner in which her teenage daughter was dressed, her response was, "that's the way I use to dress and I see nothing wrong with it," of course that was the end of that argument. However, I was not surprise when not too long after that encounter the same teenager was pregnant, and you guessed it right, dropped out of school. This is a challenge to parents, consider what you are doing to your daughters, are you encouraging them to be modest or are you teaching them immorality?

Do they have to wear the latest fashion designs?

Do you want your daughter to dress in such a way to get the boys attention and then flirt with them?

Do you want older men noticing her with anything but a clean mind? As followers of Jesus Christ we are to pursue not just physical purity, but mental, emotional, and spiritual purity as well. We are to protect our young girls from vulnerability to unhealthy and premature relationships.

Who is in charge here? "I cannot control what she wears," funny how some parents will turn a blind eye to their teenager's closets. We have to be secure enough in our duty as parent to exercise that control. If you feel your teenagers are calling the shots then you need a check up either with the family counselor or the pastor.

Let me remind you, they do not have to wear what their friends are wearing, teach them to lead and not to follow. Think about this for a moment, if your daughters look to others to determine things for her as to what she should wear then very soon she will likely having others determining what to do in other areas of her life. She will be more likely to follow the crowd into sexual compromise. Teach them to blaze their own trails through life-one that will lead them into a life of purity and godliness.

Lessons that will last a lifetime. As parent, it worth the fight to control your girls in their formative years, what they buy and what they wear when they leave the house. It seems so much easier just to give them freedom to make their own choices and hope for the best but you would be neglecting your God-given responsibilities. The same could be said for many other parts of their lives. It would be easier just to leave them and let them do their own thing, but you take them to church because you want them to have a personal relationship with the Lord and a good education from school, not just because it is the right thing to do but because you want them to be successful in fulfilling their dreams. So then, you make church and education a priority.

Every struggle you endure is worthy; you want to see them with a sense of pride in how they present themselves to others, to enjoy the respect of peers and adults, and to attract like minded friends with healthy relationships at the right time. Since you are reading this book, I know by now that you want to develop the strongest character traits in your girls, you are not alone. Theses lessons on modesty will guide them not only through puberty but for a life time.

2. Responsibilities of Older women to younger women.

Titus 2.4-5. *"that they may teach the young women to be sober, to love their husbands, to love their children. To be discreet, chaste, keepers at home, good, obedient to their own husbands, that the word of God be not blasphemed."*

When was the last time you heard this passage of Scripture read in church or a sermon taken from it? You see, we do not want to ruffle any feathers within the ranks. Older women are to teach the younger (married) women to be good stewardesses, loving, kind and tender hearted to their husbands.

In these days and times, wives and husbands have different bank accounts, most of the times these are encouraged by their mothers or older female friends, if you were to enquire for the reason for this you will hear, "just in case." So what has happened to the oneness that they became?

Paul gives these instructions as to how a young married woman is to live; train the younger women to love their husbands and children, to be self-controlled and pure, to be busy at home, to be kind and to be subject to their own husbands so that no one will malign the Word of God. It is clear that when children are in the picture, which is where the young woman's responsibilities lie.

The older women are to live and practice a life of purity so that the younger women will adapt these principles, the end results is the glorification of God. Do not listen to the world of the Feminist Movement, most of the members do not have a family and their views are worlds away from that of the Christians. The picture that people should see in your homes as they look at your family structure should bring glory to God with a view of drawing themselves closer to Christ.

Selected Scriptures

- I Timothy 2:9-10
- Titus 2:4-5

Chapter 17

Godly Parent Make a Big Difference

Choose you this day whom ye will serve; whether the gods which your fathers served that were on the other side of the flood, or the gods of the Amorites, in whose, land ye dwell. But for me and my house, we will serve the Lord. (Joshua 24:15)

The quality of life influences every part of our daily lives. Researchers have found that Americans' greatest source of happiness in life is in the family. On the other hand frustrations and disappointments are the greatest obstacles in people's life while handling family problems.

People across the world have become alarmed at the decline and decay of the family unit. In large number our families are different from others:
1. Fathers are working while mothers keep home.
2. Fathers and Mothers are both working
3. More parents are single.

4. Second marriages unions are bringing up children from unrelated background.
5. Unmarried couples are bringing up children.
6. Gays are fighting for the rights to parenthood.
7. Gays and lesbians are parents
8. Couples are childless.

We are witnessing some of the most profound and historic period in ancient history in the American family life. Some of the things, which were once forbidden, are now openly displayed and practice right before our eyes. The only ones who suffer are the children.

What Joshua said is right, "As for me and my house we will serve the Lord" the man was speaking for his family with no hidden agenda, a bold man, a God fearing man, a man who loved his family. How many men can stand up today and make this statement?

Many may not be able to make this or similar statement but all can make a difference in diverse ways. One of the ways is "prayer" Christians are admonished to pray. There are many benefits in praying, an awesome weapon used by Jesus Himself and continued by His disciples. So then, if Jesus prayed how much more should we pray especially in such a time as this.

As praying Christian parents, we can all make a big difference in our parenting method, if you do not have a prayer life, here are some ways to start one.
- Find a quiet place where you can go everyday.
- Read Scripture. You may want to start with the Book of Psalm or the Gospel of St.John.
- After reading the Scriptures, spent some time on reflections before the Lord.
- Ask the Lord to protect your family, in their going out and coming in.
- Close your prayer time with a time of praise, giving thanks for who God is and what He has done for you.
- Make this a commitment and be commitment to it.

You will be surprise how God works in your life and the differences you can make for you and your family. Be aware that God inhabits the praises of His people.

Selected Scriptures

- Joshua 24:15

Chapter 18

How a God fearing family should function.

It is always good for a child to grow up in a Christian home, where family prays and constantly read the Bible, however, it is also good that the child is encourage to be a Christian. Consider this; there is a difference between growing up in a Christian home and being a Christian-a huge difference.

Relations must be a pattern after God.

A Christian family is a family where relationships with each other are pattern after the manner of Jesus Christ. It must be a place where grace is not only extended but also demonstrated, where truth lives out and not merely talked about.

A healthy Christian home provides an atmosphere of support, encouragement and positive opportunities for growth, which includes helping each other to come to a knowledge and acceptance of God and Jesus Christ.

My father did not merely tell us how important Biblical teachings were; he took us to Church where we could learn on our own. He listened to Christian radio programs and even secular radio programs too, but he knew the difference. There was no doubt he knew, we knew too.
- When we were wrong he corrected us.
- When we were disobedient he disciplined us.
- When we sinned, he reminded us of the need to seek repentance.
- When we forgot, he reminded us.
- When we made mistakes he forgave us.
- When we are weak, he helped us to be strong.
- When I was ashamed to take a bold step, he did not belittle me, but encouraged me and listened to me and helped me to overcome, he loved and cherished me.
- He did not believe in failure, he made us strong from day to day. Thank God for Godly parents.

My Pastor, Dr.D. Holness, is famous for using this quotation, "Children live What They Learn:"
- If a child lives with criticism, he learns to condemn.
- If a child lives with hostility, he learns to fight.
- If a child lives with shame, he learns to feel guilty.
- If a child lives with tolerance, he learns to be patient.
- If a child lives with ridicule, he learns to be shy.
- If a child lives with encouragement, he learns confidence.
- If a child lives with fairness, he learns justice.
- If a child lives with security, he learns to have faith.
- If a child lives with approval, he learns to like himself.
- If a child lives with acceptance and friendship, he learns to find love in the world.

Chapter 19

Are the Children really our Future?

The children of today are indeed the next generation, they are the future, all these are expressions used by people around the world. By eloquent speakers at graduations, special functions, and fund raising events even politicians uses these lines to gain fame or to win the hearts and votes of those who will listen.

It is an exciting experience to watch a young high school student preparing him/herself to achieve ultimate goals by visiting libraries or doing research on the internet, the extra classes for SAT and ACT and the countless overtime they put into making sure that their time and lives will be benefiting and useful in the future. Then when the big day finally comes and you sit proudly in the auditorium and watch that student walk up to collect that certificate with honors and hear the speaker mention what an asset that child was to the school, you can't help but feel your heart swell with pride even though he may not be your child.

Then there is the point where the successful businessman is called upon to encourage and share past experiences and it is in this breath he proclaims that he believes the children are the future.

Now, be real, tell me where you see them being the future if we keep on neglecting them, because we cannot afford a simple computer and the basic learning tools for them. Until we start to take a page out of the books of the Jews, our children will be left behind.

Where do you see a future with the children left in their own care and protection? Where do you see a future when the fathers are in jail and the mothers wandering in the streets looking for handouts? Don't you know that it is difficult to learn if you are not taught! Until parent start to take serious care and responsibility of their children the jails will remain overcrowded.

So then, this writer truly believes that the children are our future, the following must be true of us.
- We must pray for them and with them.
- We must provide for their every need.
- We must love them.
- We must respect them
- We must not put them down
- We must not called them names
- We must be there for them
- We must respect their rights, yes they have rights too.
- We must bring them up in the way of the Lord.

Chapter 20

Children don't come with Manuals. (Instructions)

For a while this writer has been thinking on this phrase once heard on The Oprah Winfrey Show, "Children don't come with Instructions."

This is so true, they do not come with manuals or instructions and as such, there are people in the world who have no idea what to do with them.

One such person is the mother I saw a few days ago with three children, all between the ages of 2 and 7 years, with no food for them she was just hoping a Good Samaritan would come to her rescue. Now, she has no business being a mother. In fact, she has no business having sex, but we cannot control that part, sadly. However, we can do something to fix the parenting habit.

Here is how; since mothers like the one mentioned are dependent on others or government to provide basic amenities for children, then government should institute a testing system to see who should and should not become parents.

This test should take the form of a psychological form in which one is assess in the qualities and personalities of parenting. The result of these tests should determine who would be parents.

We take test and examinations for almost every thing in this world before we can be qualified as professionals, then why not for the most important thing as parenting?

This is the most important job of our life, yet we are allowed to do just that "like that"

As a result some women are having children who have no business being near them. Once upon a time, the more children they have determines how much money they receive from government but the ride is over.

How many times can you remember mothers and grandmothers leaving children in hot cars, just to do personal business only to returned and find these young innocent ones dead by heat strokes.

How can a mother forget her baby? She carried it for nine months, had to undergo great pains and then forget them. Were the testing system in place, we would not be arguing about this now, because if some of these mothers were found unfit they would be warned and should they go and still become mothers then the children would be taken away.

Don't leave your children home alone to go partying, if you have no one to care for them, then guess what, you don't go.

Children are children, not mini adults, yet some of us think it is cute to pierce our son's ears and dress our young daughters like adults then we are the first ones to blame some men for their actions, not remembering that we helped them to become what they should not have been until later.

We must endeavor to encourage our men and women to become more sexual prudent. Too many of our men have this sad belief that to be "real men" requires one to have many offspring, often with as many women as possible, absolute rubbish. If this is what it takes to be a man, then maybe we all should stay in the boyhood state.

In respect to our women, too many of them rather carelessly and foolishly go about having children with each man with whom they have a relationship, under the rather false belief that giving each man a child will make him love and stay with her. Wake up women, stop dreaming.

We must start from early to poise the minds of our young men in our societies the importance of parenting, to make them to understand and appreciate the real significance to their complete involvement as parent. We may be able to adjust a sad cultural practice and probably make a difference in our society.

This writer was caught up in an argument once, the conversation was about how to support children, not one of the participants once mention spending quality time with their children.

Finances were the dominant theme, money is essential, but it is not all. As men we should not be only "sperm donors" or one who never spend quality time with the child we help to create.

As a male, at times I feel disappointed in my gender, to see how some of us treat our children and by extension the mothers. We believe that showing some care and sharing some pains will make us soft.

I am also disappointed to know that some men have to be force by law to add their names to his child's birth certificate and pay child support. If you did not have a problem laying with the mother then you should not have a problem supporting that which both of you created.

Children are born innocent and became what they learn, at home, at school and beyond. By paying attention and caring now, the future, as dark as it may seem, just might become a better place.

Chapter 21

Taking Parenthood Seriously

Now with all seriousness, look around you at the indiscipline, the raggedness, the coarseness, crudity and violence which have become an integral part of our society, this just jumps out right at you. This by the way is not unique to this society but is true in almost every where you go and I wish I could say differently but it is not getting better anytime soon.

One day a few years ago, while working at my business place in Atlanta, I saw a teenage girl pushing a baby carriage with a toddler in it. This girl was obviously very pregnant couldn't have been more than eighteen years old. Right then, something struck me, it was the thought of "the difficulty" which young people have to experience and endure. Especially those who are the minorities. In this modern, ultra-competitive society, why should a young person want to burden herself with the difficult task of parenting in her formative years? Robbing and denying themselves of their youthful days, there are so many things to enjoy in those years, College, friends and others.

As a youngster, I have heard on many occasions the older folks lamented about the importance of standing tall in the community. Teenage pregnancy was not one of the important things to make one tall. These days, children are been produced by single parents like it is going out of style.

As the proverb says, it's easy to become a parent, but it is a whole entirely different thing in being one.

We can all cite some examples of children whose parents did everything for them, yet they turned out to be no good. And yet we wonder about the ones who were left pretty much to wander around because father was a distance presence or of no consequence in their lives, mother did all she could in an unfriendly environment to survive. The end result, the phenomenon leaves us with a bunch of dysfunctional people who can contribute only minimally to their own survival and to the society in general. In extreme cases, they turn out to be hardened and vicious criminals with the desire of creating havoc in people's lives.

Things did not have to come to this, but because of lack of proper parenting, no one saw the need to take parenting seriously. Many fathers believe that if things are working there is no needs to fix them, if he can get milk for free why bother to buy the cow. So then the question of commitment is thrown out the window, not realizing that this same child is watching and taking lessons from mother and father.

It is easy to lament about the "good old days" when things were "so much better". Well. Those days were not necessarily better; they were merely simpler. They had their own drawbacks as well, life was rigid, narrowly focused and circumscribed, and governed by a passion of love and survival. The distractions were fewer, leaving parents with the ability to devote more time and efforts to the development of their children. Attentions were a priority; as such many of those children managed to grow up and developed into productive well balanced human beings.

Amid the disorder and disarray today, you can still see the effects of those who make the efforts and concentrate on the difficult, demanding, day-to-day sacrifice of raising their children into decent, self-respecting, productive citizens. These are the one who are holding up the four walls, the parents of course are the foundation.

They continue to make solid structure that keeps society functioning, even among all the battering and buffeting of the awesome forces at work in the world.

Can you remember when your mothers used to pray for and with you? Yes, that was then, don't you think it time to get back to the heavenly places by going on our knees and ask God for deliverance? Can't we devise some way of requiring people to pass an exam and obtain a license before they are allowed to have children? I think the time has arrived, if we don't, things definitely will get worse than better. As the older folks used to say "this is only the brush, the currycomb is coming."

Notes

Chapter 22

Defiling our Children

Most if not all of the entertainment industry is overflowing with erotica, sexually aggressive "dancing" soap -opera romance, gratuitous sex and violence. Reports of death and carnage bombarded and desensitize innocent young minds daily. Aggression, dishonesty, and uncultured behavior are constantly served up on the streets, in our communities and in the homes. As a result, children therefore become tainted and susceptible.

Children of all classes indulge in early sexual intercourse. Crowded communities and poverty only make things worse. Pregnancies and poverty have a direct relationship: they also perpetuate each other. As a general rule the greater the poverty the less the education and the less education the less prospect for a career.

The bearing of children therefore becomes a matter of course. Poor people have little or no income and no retirement benefits coming to them. Their progeny become the source of support from the baby fathers.

Children should be children, when was the last time you see children playing hopscotch, ring games or telling stories? Now children play at being adults and in so doing they bypass the one essential ingredient for their wholesome development, childhood.

Since we cannot sequester all our children, our society must review the practice of using sex and sex objects to promote music, movies and other productions. Sex is natural but society's exploitation of it has precipitated a deluge of unhealthy ideation and practices.

What then are we to expect from our children? They certainly deserve better.

Chapter 23

Raising Up or Growing Up.

Children these days are classified as unruly, dangerous and other things other than being nice. The folks who are complaining are mostly parents, teachers and those who have contacts with kids.

The big question is "are kids being raise up or grow up?" You see there was a time when children were raised up, certainty not these days. No sir- ree, these kids just grow up. They figure out stuff all by themselves, regardless of the consequences that follows. They are confused, insecure and sometimes violent.

If one should draw a parallel between kids and plants, many kids of the past would be like roses. Attention were paid to them, they were watered, well molded and fed with tender care until they were ready to meet the challenges of the outside world. In contrast, today's kids are growing up wild and uncultured.

In my formative years, the entire community of Mt. Pleasant participated in the children's upbringing. Teachers, shopkeepers, pastors, and farmers even the bread salesman (Mass Percy) all saw to it that children remain at their best behavior at all times.

In the event where a kid was misbehaving, you can be assured that your parents were going to hear about it and a whipping of a life time is sure to follow depending on the nature of the crime. You would be fortunate if you did not get one before you reach home.

Misconduct in school was a no; no, because the teachers were given authority to make adjustments and corrections for minor infractions should you decide to violate the code of conduct. And if word should ever get back to your parents that your teacher or anyone else had to punish you, there would be no question that your first correction would be repeated when you get home.

These days, teachers can't even talk loudly to a student much more to administer punishment. Kids are taking guns and other dangerous weapons to schools, parents are ready to defend their boisterous and unruly behavior even before the facts are known as to the truth of any involvement. All these and more came about as a result of parents allowing their children to grow up instead of raising them up.

These days when a child has committed a crime he/she is told to go to their room, the same room with a television set, the same television set which has cable with BET and MTV to name a few. Go figure, the fact that our children, who are unable to tell the difference between right or wrong have no guidance are being grown up by television is not only disturbing but outright frightening.

So the room with the television becomes the class rooms and based upon what I know about those channels, intelligent knowledge seldomly come from that form of teaching.

I hope you are not still wondering why so many teachers are leaving the classrooms, would you work under those conditions where you are unable to discipline today's ignorant, violent, unruly and disrespectful kids without coming into direct confrontation with ignorant, violent and disrespectful parents and fearful of school administrations? For what incentive? I wouldn't.

This writer will challenge today's parents to do the math, if they can, because I am sure that many of them are not able to do much better than their kids. If teachers are scared to do their jobs and your kids are unable to read because of your behavior and the time they spent with video games and TV and you don't ensure that they spend time reading and completing assignments something worthwhile, what do you expect of them, miracle?

Well here is the reality, Jesus and His disciples were the real miracles workers on earth and they have been gone now for more than two thousand years.

Notes

Chapter 24

Taking a Manly Stand.

This writer have learned that there is a difference between being "the Man and being A Man." I found this out later in my life. You see, I was taught that being "the Man" was the way to go, being a man was ridicule and openly criticized by my peers. After coming to the knowledge of truth and sensibility it dawned on me that "being the man "always had something to prove and someone to prove it to.

The man is expected to prove his worth by having a lot of women to be promiscuous; he had to have a lot of girls, not just to pose with them but to have children by all of them.

The pressure to measure up and be the Man was a heavy burden; nevertheless, I played the role.

Then one day I asked myself, why?

There were no good reason for having so many women-except to beat my chest and echoed respect from my close friends. The rationale I could come up with was not being able to trust women, but then; I knew not all women had the same traits.

Ironically, wanting to change the habits is when I was in the prime of my young agile life, with popularity that all my peers craved. Nevertheless it was during this time that I have decided to change from "being the Man and be a Man."

One night I sat down and reminisced about the many gallons of tears that I have caused to flow from the hearts of many young ladies who have ventured in my path, all in the name of being the Man. After becoming a man, I was severely criticized and ridiculed but I stood my grounds without faltering. Under severe pressure to return to my olds ways, I realize that being "A Man" took a lot of courage and character; I fell on few occasions but never return to my old ways. Eventually, most of my peers respected my decision and confessed that they too will follow my path very soon.

Being 'the Man' one has to possession of a gun, smoke, drink and other traits like that, however, being "A Man" requires fundamental respect to foster care for his wife and children. This is what God requires from us. Many who attempt to be "the Man" are not here today to read this book.

Departure from being "the Man" was the first step with a long walk to being "A Man" many years ago I made the biggest step in the direction of being a servant of the Lord, now He is in charge of making me "A Man" the one He wants me to be.

Chapter 25

Faithful Partners (Dating a Married Man)

From a Christian perspective, there are absolutely no good reasons for dating a married man. Even the reasons you though were good don't stand the test of time and turn out to be bad ideas masquerading as good ones. Should you find your self on the brink of temptation, take a look at these facts carefully before you get involve.

- **He will not commit to a future with you.** "Never mind the wife it's you I really love, or the I've never felt this way before. A man who is in an unhappy or unsatisfying marriage can feel swept away by how wonderful you make him feel. This may sound like a commitment to a future with you, but it is not. Do not confuse his loving the way you make him feel with the loving you enough to make a commitment to you.
- **He's got his cake and eat it too.** He has the security of a legitimate (his marriage) that help his public persona and the excitement of an illegitimate one with you to make up for what he's missing in his marriage.

- **Hiding is exhausting**. There are places you cannot go and things you cannot do together. You must not think so at the beginning but having to keep your relationship a secret can affect your self-esteem, moreover you will be left out on all wonderful and special occasions.
- Cheating tell how he deals with difficult situations. You are evidence of how he avoids dealing with difficult situations head on. This means that he's also likely to resort to some devious action if and when the two of you encounter relational problems.
- **You are only fooling around.** Irrespective of his assurances about how much you means to him, by not ending his relationship with his wife in an above –board respectfully and not legalizing his relationship with you is really a testimony of how much he thinks of you. Actions speak louder than words. Stop wasting your time. You deserve better than putting up with someone else's leftovers. So the loving is good, but remember that it was the forbidden fruit got Eve in trouble.
- **Can you love someone who disrespects his wife**? The existence of your relationship with a married man tells you how little his wife means to him and the amount of respect he has for her.
- **You are not only a home wrecker, you are also an Accomplice**. Like it or not, you are a willing participant in a man violating his marriage vows made between God and man. Just think of the children, who will end up being the victims.
- **It is just plain adultery**. The penalty for adultery in the Old Testament was death; you are a guilty party in an adulterous affair which is a sin.

Chapter 26

Legacy of Parents

Your statutes are my heritage for ever; they are the joy of my heart. Psalm 119:111

You may not be aware of this, children receives something from parents. It is called heritage. If you were asked to define what will your children inherit from you, what would be your answer? Unfortunately as it may be, many are unclear what it really is! Here is a definition, "a heritage is the spiritual, emotional and social legacy that is passed down from parent to their children... favorable or unfavorable."

A legacy on the other hand is something resulting from, and followed by, an action, person or event.

As it is mentioned in the definition, a heritage has three parts; they are related and stronger with all elements together. It is geared to strengthen us as we modeled our parent's good deeds, it gives stability for the present and future life, it also gives hope for a better tomorrow.

The spiritual: In modern times, most parents are planning for a financial future for their children and forgetting their spiritual needs. This is the most neglected part of the family structure. Most of the times this occurs as a result of the life modeled in the home. Other times good Christian values were modeled but children just ended up being socially inept and chose the worldly standards rather the Christian values.

The Emotional. This influences the spiritual and social as well. This lasting legacy was molded in the safe confines of the home where everyone enjoys a measure of love and self worth. One cannot deny the fact that many children experienced great amount of emotional depressions, but this too will manifest in them in time to come. However, strong emotional values are encouraged for all. Children need an environment in which they are free to learn how to experience or express their God-given emotions. The life of Christ is the perfect example for our children.

In His humanity, Jesus experienced grief, compassion, sympathy, love, and anger. In all of this He did not commit any sin but continued to do His Father's will.

Selected Scriptures

- Psalm 119:111

Notes

Chapter 27

Bringing the Family Back

There is an urgent need for an international campaign, reformation, and transformation to rebuild the family unit. This could be called "Bringing the family back" and would rely heavily on the Christian churches, schools and mass media to teach and educate people on the sacredness and sanctity of life.

The First and Second Great Awakenings were direct campaigns to bring people back to the basics, which was taught and practiced by their forefathers. With great results and success spiritual worship and family values were once again common place.

This reformation and campaign would awaken the consciences of the population to the following,
- The existence of God.
- The awesome responsibilities to our children and communities.

- To encourage people to know and practice their civic duties.
- To teach young men to be more responsible.
- To teach young people to be more tolerant.
- To teach young people that it is O.K to learn to agree to disagree with each other.
- To encourage young people to put off having babies until they can afford to be responsible parents.
- To teach parents to love each other even in the midst of trials and tribulations.
- To remind parents of their marriage vows.
- To encourage parents to be good examples for their children.

Parents would also encourage in creating an atmosphere of love within homes where each child is taught the values and morals of his life and of others.

Since realistically all people will not be married, here, I am not an advocate for single parents, then those who do not live with their children should create the atmosphere for others to be a part of their children's lives. An important role of fathers, not only as financial supplier but to give solid emotional support.

This reformation and campaign should be centered upon the parents' moreso, because when parents are convinced of their responsibilities, the broader society, including churches, schools and media houses could follow suits and help to teach values and attitudes. By taking these importance steps, our communities would see a drastic change.

It must also be known that there is a fundamental role that the broader society cannot offer; however, this role can be offered in the homes. As such, values and attitudes must be taught in the home. It is not possible to be disrespectful at home and be respectful out side the home.

The end result from this reformation and campaign would be enormous. Predictably, we should evolve into a more genteel, loving and peace society, where people can once again be human beings, loving and caring for each other as were the case long time ago.

Society would also become more productive and crime and violence would be of the past.

The time for this reformation and campaign is now to bring back the family to its former glory and let it begin with me. As a parent I am willing to do whatever it takes to get the family right for a peaceful and better tomorrow. Parents should not sit by and allow society to continue like business as usual. The eyes of the Lord are upon us. The responsibilities are great but, do not lose heart, God is also a great God. So as Sergeant Friday would say, "That's just the facts mam." Let's bring the family back.

References

Ahrons, C.R. The effect of the post divorce relationship on paternal establishment and child support. **Social Science Review**. 1993. Pp 72, 109-126

Baker, G. & Brown, Janet. Head of the Caribbean Child Development Center.

Belsky, L & Volling, B.L. Mothering, Fathering and Marital Interaction in the family triad during infancy. **Men's transitions to Parenthood: Longitudinal studies of early family experience**. 1987. Pp 37-63. Hillsdale, NJ.

Furstenberg, F.F. & Nord, C.W. Parenting apart; Pattern of childrearing after marital disruption. **Journal of Marriage and the Family**. 1987. Pp. 47, 893-904.

Lewis, Robert. Raising a Modern-Day Knight. 1954.

The Oprah Winfrey Show.

King James Version. **Bible**

About the Author

Dr. Robert H. Givons was born in the beautiful Island of Jamaica, WI in a little village called Mt. Pleasant in the parish of Manchester.

He accepted the Lord Jesus Christ as his personal savior at the Coffee Grove Church of God and was baptized at an early age.

After leaving High School in Porus, Manchester he enlisted in the Jamaica Constabulary Force (JCF) where he served with distinctions and honors for eight years. (Achieving the rank of Detective Corporal of Police).

In 1985 he migrated to New York, USA. Where he studied Computer Science in Hempstead NY.

Dr. Givons is currently serving as an Associate pastor at the Central Christian Church in Atlanta, Ga.

After being called to the ministry he attended the Carver Bible College where he earned a Bachelor of Arts degree in Biblical Studies.

Then went on to Luther Rice University to pursue a Master of Divinity degree.

After that it was on to Jacksonville Theological Seminary (JTS) for a doctor of ministry degree (D.Min) (Class of 2006).

He owns and operates a computer service center in Atlanta for the past fifteen years.

He is the author of a book entitled, "Parenting from a Biblical Perspective" which will be published next fall.

He is married with four children and currently residing in Atlanta, Georgia. US.

Robert Givons can be reach by email at Rgivons@aol.com.

Printed in the United States
72760LV00007B/46-93